Meeting the Needs of Transient Students

by
Donovan R. Walling

Library of Congress Catalog Card Number 90-60212
ISBN 0-87367-304-2
Copyright © 1990 by the Phi Delta Kappa Educational Foundation
Bloomington, Indiana

This fastback is sponsored by the Redding California Chapter of Phi Delta Kappa, which made a generous contribution toward publication costs.

21479159

Table of Contents

Introduction

America is a nation on the move — literally. About 20% of the population moves each year, including many families with school-age children. Uprooting of families takes its toll on children as they attempt to cope with the stress of moving. For transient children to succeed in school, we must, first of all, help them to acquire membership in the school community.

Human beings are social creatures, children no less so than adults. We have a strong need to belong to a group or a community. How we see ourselves as individuals — our self-concept — is determined largely by how well we are accepted by the group. We define ourselves by the groups in which we hold membership. We are by turns Americans, New Yorkers, Texans, north-siders, Rotarians, military children.

The word community comes from the Latin word *communis*, meaning "in common" or "shared." A community — a neighborhood, a school — is composed of members who share values and experiences. They hold a common outlook, belong to a common culture, and adhere to a common norm. Communities protect individuals against loneliness and alienation. Like the walled cities of the Middle Ages, communities are strongholds against the unknowns of the outside world. Community membership is a powerful force for security and self-worth — a force driven by a sense of belonging.

Moving disrupts community membership. When people move from one city to another, from one state to another, they abandon the community that has supported them psychologically and physically. Now they must attempt to join a new one. "Attempt" is the key word here. People who move to new communities must change in ways — sometimes subtle, sometimes dramatic — that make them eligible for membership. They must adapt to a new set of norms. If they do not, they will be kept out of the community — at least psychologically.

Psychological exclusion is not unlike the "shunning" practiced by certain religious groups. Historically, some groups have shunned members as a way of punishing them for violations of group norms. "Sinful" members are neither looked at nor spoken to for a period of repentance. Other communities react similarly to transgressors of group norms. The neighbor with the rusted-out automobile on the front lawn in a neat, middle-class community is not likely to have many friends on the street.

For children, a move of even a few blocks within the same city may disrupt their sense of belonging, because their communities are much smaller than those of adults. Perception of self emerges from interaction with other children in a cultural context. When moving displaces the familiar culture, children are forced to adapt to a new culture. When moving occurs frequently, the demands of adaptation may be more than the child can manage successfully without help.

In order to meet the needs of transient children in school, educators must help them to learn as soon as possible the ways of the new school culture and to feel that they belong to this culture. This is important for any child who moves and especially so for those who move often.

This fastback examines the problems of transient children and suggests ways the school can help them cope with the "culture shock" of moving.

Moving and Being

Moving is stressful for most people — children and adults alike — not simply because of the physical changes that relocation entails but more so because of the psychological adjustments that mobile people must make. Of course, everyone who moves has to cope with a myriad of physical details: finding a new home, perhaps a new job, arranging for transportation of the family, contacting a moving company, and so on. The stress parents feel when coping with these details is transmitted to their children. But there are more subtle, psychological adjustments that children must make, whether they are elementary, middle, or high school age.

Children who move are concerned with fundamental questions of being. Will I be accepted as I am? Will I fit in? Will I be able to make new friends? Will people like me? And, underlying these questions is the fundamental concern: Will I still be me? Moving to a new community means adjusting to a new set of norms and values.

To meet the affective needs of students who move, educators need to understand the psychological phenomena of moving. A good place to begin is with some basic questions: Who moves? And why?

Who Moves and Why?

Nearly one of every five persons in the United States will move this year. In fact, according to U.S. Census Bureau records, about

20% of Americans over the age of one have moved each year since 1948, when mobility statistics were first recorded. Mobility reached an all-time low of 16.6% in 1982-83, but it has been on the rise ever since.

This means that more than 40 million people are on the move each year in this country. Some are young adults seeking employment or relocating for other job-related reasons. Others are retirees – although in fewer numbers than popularly imagined. Many are families with school-age children.

People who move can be classified in several categories. In terms of social class, for example, professional people with high incomes are more likely to move than those in the middle of the social scale. They tend to move farther, too. Vance Packard reported this trend in his influential 1972 book, *A Nation of Strangers*. The trend has not changed in recent years.

At the opposite end of the social scale are those who are unemployed. They also are above-average movers, but they move shorter distances usually. Working-class (or middle-class) people move least often. Stronger local neighborhood ties, fewer skills for coping with change, and less opportunity to relocate within the job market are reasons cited for this group's relative stability.

Generalizations about mobility and social class, however, must be tempered by other factors. For example, take occupation. Independent professionals, such as doctors and dentists, do not move often. Established practices are difficult to relocate or re-establish. Engineers who work for large corporations, on the other hand, are sometimes very mobile, frequently relocating to new job sites. Moving companies report that nearly three-fourths of all the people they move long distances are employed by large corporations or by the government.

One type of mobile government employee is a member of the armed services. Military personnel constitute one of the most mobile segments of the U.S. population. Military families are frequently on the move, involving nearly two million children. These children live on or near military installations across the nation and around the globe.

The standard cycle of military mobility is three years, although personnel tend to move more often during the early years of their careers. Military children may transfer among the many installation-based schools, but frequently there are also periods when they attend local "civilian" schools. Figure 1 shows an actual profile of mobility for a military child that is quite typical. In 12 years of schooling, this student changed schools 10 times. Length of stay in any single school ranged from a low of only four months to a high of two years and two months. What Figure 1 does not show is that this student experienced twelve changes of housing during the same years. The additional moves resulted when the family was forced to live in temporary military quarters or civilian apartments while awaiting a vacancy in official or permanent housing.

Age is another factor in mobility. Persons between 25 and 35 are the most frequent movers, regardless of occupation. This is also the age group that is most likely to have young, school-age children. Some studies show that families with elementary school children are more likely to move than those with high school-age children. This is particularly true if the parents regard the potential negative effect on an adolescent as a primary factor in their decision to move or not move.

The 25-35 age group is also more apt to rent than to own a home. Related studies using type of dwelling as a variable factor have shown that renters are more likely to move — and to move more often — than those who own their homes. People who buy a house usually intend to stay put, at least for a longer time.

Two mobile groups with very special needs are migrants and immigrants, particularly refugees. Migrant workers have been called the "invisible people." They labor in fields not far from urban centers, and yet few city-dwellers are aware of their existence. They live in labor camps located on large truck farms or orchards out of sight, or they live in the run-down neighborhoods that most people avoid. They tend to move themselves instead of hiring a moving company.

Figure 1. Mobility Profile of a Typical Military Child.

Grade	Type of School	Reason for Relocation
1	Civilian (4 months)	Father re-assigned; child did not attend kindergarten in previous locations.
	Military (5)	Father re-assigned to new geographic location in U.S.
2	No change	
3	Civilian (9)	Students were bused to off-post school because of overcrowded conditions at the post elementary school.
4	Military (9)	Overcrowding was relieved; student returned to post school.
5	Civilian (4)	Father sent overseas; family moved to different state temporarily, until overseas family housing became available.
	Military (5)	Family moved overseas to join father.
6	No change	
7	Military (5)	Father was re-assigned to a new location within the same overseas command area (country).
	Military (4)	Father was re-assigned again to a third overseas location.
8	Civilian (9)	Family returned to the U.S.
9	No change (7)	
	Military (2)	Family moved back overseas to last location noted in previous overseas tour of duty.
10	No change	
11	No change	
12	Military (9)	Family returned to U.S. during August-September; student entered new school 2-3 weeks late.

Migrant workers move seasonally to follow the crops. Their children often attend school for only a few weeks in the same place. Many times the children are absent from school, kept home to take care of younger siblings or at work in the fields with their parents in spite of child labor laws prohibiting such work. Migrant children often come from non-English-speaking families. Language problems hamper their attempts to succeed in school. (See fastback 145 *Migrant Education: Teaching the Wandering Ones* by Joyce King-Stoops.)

The same language barriers exist almost universally for immigrants, many of whom also work as migrants. However, immigrants who are not migrant workers also tend to be mobile, at least during the period immediately following arrival in the United States. They are often poor or unemployed. They move to find work, but as often as not they move to a community where their friends and relatives who preceded them live. Southeast Asian refugees — Vietnamese, Hmong, Cambodian, and others — tend to cluster in cities where other members of their culture have settled. Often rejected or ignored by mainstream society because of cultural and linguistic differences, immigrant children in school are torn between maintaining the traditions of their parents or abandoning their parents' ways in order to fit into the adoptive culture. Mexican, Nicaraguan, and other Latin American immigrants face similar conflicts in schools and neighborhoods.

Positive and Negative Relocations

Yet another perspective for considering mobility is the child's attitude toward a move. How children feel about a move is affected by how their parents view the move. If the move is seen as positive by the parents, then children usually feel less anxious. The move may bring career advancement. It may mean better pay or a better home. The move may be to a climate or locale that the parents view more positively. If the parents eagerly look forward to the move, chances are favorable that the children will, too.

On the other hand, if parents see the move negatively, then the children are likely to be more anxious about moving. An involuntary transfer may be a step down in status or salary. The move may take the family away from friends and relatives to an undesirable location or simply to a place the parents do not want to live. The move may be a response to losing a job.

Negative attitudes that parents communicate about the move affect how their children view the move. But the move may also result in additional stress for children, because some children blame themselves for their parents' negative feelings. A child may wonder, Am I the cause of this problem? When children are on the receiving end of short tempers during the tensions of moving, they can and do assume that they are at least partly to blame.

Family configuration is another consideration. The fact that both parents work in many families can cause additional conflict. In terms of career goals, a move may affect one parent positively and the other negatively. Dual-career families are increasing in number. For example, in military families, where traditionally wives have not been employed outside the home, the increase in dual-careers has been dramatic. Between 1970 and 1980, the numbers of working military wives rose from 30.5% to 50.3% (Pisano 1982).

Career advancement that calls for the transfer of one parent may put the other parent's career on hold or end it completely. Stress caused by conflicting career goals related to a move also affects children's feelings. With which parent should their sympathies lie? Are they to blame for the conflict?

Single-parent families feel additional stress with a move because there is no other adult with whom to share the responsibilities. Younger children in these families may find themselves in some different child-care arrangement in order for the parent to handle all the details involved with moving. Older children may be left more often to care for themselves during the move. Even in families with two parents, one parent's absence for an extended period for house-hunting or job-hunting can cause a feeling in children that all is not well.

Regardless of family configuration, disruption and uncertainty are an inevitable part of moving. How parents view the move is a key factor in either increasing or decreasing their children's anxieties.

How Children Feel About Moving

It is easy for parents to overlook or ignore their children's feelings in the turmoil of a move. The stresses of moving can lead children to believe that something is wrong in the family. Sometimes this results in feelings of guilt and unworthiness, which only compound their uncertainties about the move. These feelings are especially reinforced by the loss of their friends.

All children who move feel a sense of loss, just as adults do. That feeling of loss is both general and specific. There is the general loss of all that is familiar — home, neighborhood, school, and teachers. But the specific and most acute loss is the loss of their friends.

The losses brought about by moving may be manifested as a form of grieving. In fact, children may emotionally go through the familiar stages of grieving experienced when someone close to them dies. They may first express denial and anger at the prospect of a move, then sorrow in anticipation of their loss, and finally acceptance of the plan to move.

Parents and teachers need to understand that moving is a time of disorientation for children. Regardless of their age, children make a transition from the known to the unknown. Even if the move is viewed positively by parent and child alike, there probably will be feelings of anger and sorrow at the prospect of giving up familiar persons and surroundings.

Transition Stress

Children who are mobile may well lead what one researcher has termed a life of "strangership." Highly transient children sometimes feel as if they never truly belong anywhere. As one 18-year-old military child in the study I recently completed put it: "You have no certain home." A feeling of "strangership" is not unique to transient children, but certainly it is more likely to occur among those who move often and to persist during the relatively stable periods between moves.

The act of moving can be thought of as a cycle involving three phases: anticipation, relocation, and adjustment. This cycle is followed by a period of routine. For children who are only occasionally mobile, there are long stable periods of routine between the cycles of moving. But for children who are highly transient, the cycle of anticipation-relocation-adjustment may be perceived as nearly unending.

Vance Packard comments that "American society has an urgent need for remedies that will reduce the feeling of so many people that they are in the midst of relative strangers." Transient children especially need these remedies in order to adjust to, and obtain membership in, the new community, which will allow them to move quickly into the routine stage. The sooner children reach the stable or routine stage between cycles of moving, the sooner they can move on to academic pursuits in school.

The entire cycle of moving is fraught with anxiety for children. It is only between cycles when a normal routine is established that children can have a sense of relative certainty about their lives. The challenge for educators is to decrease the time needed for the adjustment phase of the moving cycle, so children can quickly move into the routine stage. Expediting the adjustment phase is particularly crucial for highly mobile children from military and migrant worker families.

Educators have little control over the anticipation and relocation phases of the moving cycle, but they can — and should — be sensitive to a child's need for security during the anticipation phase. It is in the adjustment phase that teachers and administrators can provide the most help in dealing with the affective needs of transient students.

Parent Uncertainties

Transition stress is a general term used to describe all the emotional upheaval associated with moving. It includes all the stress surrounding anticipating the move, relocating, and adjusting to new surroundings after the move. One special type of adjustment stress, "culture shock," will be discussed separately in the next section.

As mentioned earlier, how parents handle transition stress will affect how their children react. For all children, but especially for young ones, the mother's adjustment to the move is a critical factor. A child's adjustment to the idea of moving, to the act of relocation, and to the new community is determined to a great extent by how successfully the mother copes with the stresses of the move. This is especially true when the father is absent, because then the children have only the mother as a model of coping. Modeling is a powerful teacher at home and in school. Parents and teachers who model positive attitudes about moving impart to children positive ways to cope with the move.

Children's reactions to their parents' worries about moving are manifested in different ways. A parent may be worried about finding a new job or a new place to live, whereas the child worries about the family's disruption and wonders when the parents will be "happy" again. Or they worry about whether the new school will be "nice" and whether there will be children the same age in the neighborhood to play with. (The last time this author moved, his son's primary concern was to find a house with a basketball hoop. The fact that one could be easily installed did not ease his anxiety over finding a house with one already in place.)

Invariably, parents worry about finances involved in a move. Will the costs be more than they have budgeted? Will they have to dip into their savings? Will the rent or mortgage payments be much higher in the new location? Children sense these parent concerns, even when they are too young to understand fully the financial implications.

The Move Itself

The actual physical relocation also produces high levels of stress. Personal belongings and treasured possessions are packed into anonymous-looking boxes, loaded onto a truck by strangers, and sent off — perhaps never to be seen again. Will they actually arrive at the new home? Will things get broken?

And what about the actual transportation of the family? Will they drive across country or fly? What about staying in strange motels, eating in unfamiliar restaurants (where children are expected to be on their best behavior)? The child may wonder, What if I get sick on the airplane? Will they lose my suitcase?

Spending the first night at a new home, going to a new school for the first time, meeting strangers at every turn — all of these uncertainties are stressful, even if parents have treated the move as a grand adventure for all the family.

Loss of Significant Others

Most disruptive to a child's sense of stability and belonging is the loss of contact with significant others. Temporary parental absence is one type of loss. It is common for a parent, usually the father, to be away from the family for a time in anticipation of a move. The parent may need to look for housing or employment. A delay in selling a house may mean that one parent must stay behind while the other goes on to the new location to begin work. Children are sometimes torn between staying with one parent or the other. In the child's mind neither option is palatable. The solution is to have the move completed and the family together.

A move also may mean separation from the extended family of grandparents, aunts, and uncles. When families are close, moving away can be particularly wrenching. One 18-year-old military child in the study mentioned earlier commented: "The negative aspect [of growing up in a military family] which is highlighted in my mind is the fact of not being close to other relatives due to the constant moves."

Children will miss neighbors, teachers, and relatives outside the immediate family, of course, but it is the loss of their friends that most disturbs them at almost every age. In *The Art of Teaching Writing*, Lucy Calkins quotes a migrant worker's son Roberto: "I move so much that my dog's the only friend I have for always." Children in military families report similar feelings, sometimes with a touch of sad resignation. In the study of military children, one 17-year-old senior at a military base high school wrote: "Military children tend to be more realistic about friendships, since they are constantly moving every few years. Military children don't really attempt to get close to people."

Adolescents in particular are apt to feel the loss of friends keenly. In studies of mobile families, those parents who gave priority to their children's feelings about moving were reluctant to move during the high school years. It is generally agreed that the most difficult ages for moving are roughly 3 to 6 and 15 to 18 (early childhood and adolescence), the ages when children either require more security and stability or are more dependent on their peer group. A former military child captured the feelings of many transient children when he said: "I envy those with friends they still have from childhood."

Culture Shock

Usually, when the term "culture shock" is mentioned, people think in terms of what happens to them when traveling to foreign cultures. But culture shock also is experienced when immigrants come to the United States and when transient students move into a new neighborhood and go to a new school. A school is a culture. Moving to a new school tends to produce its own kind of culture shock.

LaRay Barna (1976) defines culture shock as a combination of emotional and physiological reactions brought about by sudden immersion in a new culture. Living in their indigenous culture shields people from the unknown and reduces the need to make choices and defend values. But sudden immersion in a new culture plunges a person — emotionally and physically — into a state of tension as he or she is confronted with new stimuli.

The tension of culture shock comes from the feeling of disorientation, a sense of being out-of-balance with the surrounding environment. To varying degrees it affects both adults and children depending on their prior experience, attitudes toward moving, and initial experiences in the new culture. Highly transient students sometimes seem less affected by culture shock than do students who are only occasionally mobile. These students may have developed coping skills during the course of frequent moves, which enable them to deal more readily with culture shock than students who move less often. But, like the student who wrote that "Military children don't really attempt to get close to people," the coping skills that transient students develop may be negative as well as positive.

Mental and Physical Symptoms

Like any ailment, culture shock has its own etiology, symptoms, and treatments. Culture shock is precipitated by the loss of familiar signs and symbols of social intercourse, the cues people use to orient themselves to situations in daily life. Knowing what questions to ask and whom to ask for answers, knowing the "system," knowing what to take seriously and what to take in jest — all of these types of knowledge are cued through social interaction within a specific cultural context. They are like familiar landmarks.

When a newcomer arrives, many of the familiar cultural landmarks may be missing. New landmarks must be found. Although schools in the United States bear many similarities, each is just a bit different from others, even if they are only on opposite sides of town.

No matter how positive students feel about moving to a new community and school, they are likely to feel that the props have been kicked out from under them the first few days or weeks of school. And they will react accordingly. At first, they may reject the new environment by resorting to statements that glorify the school they attended before. They gloss over any problems they might have had in their old school. It is as though everything good was left behind.

Other symptoms of culture shock might be heightened concern about personal hygiene and general cleanliness. New students may fear being robbed or injured. They may become absent-minded, dreamy, and overly dependent on others, particularly those students who have befriended them in the new school. They may get angry easily over small matters. And, always, they feel the gnawings of homesickness.

Stages of Adjustment

Peter Adler (1975) identified five stages of adjustment dealing with culture shock. Although his frame of reference was broader than the context of transient students, his stages are applicable to students' adjustment to a new school culture. Adler's stages, in sequence, are contact, disintegration, reintegration, autonomy, and independence.

Contact. The perception in this first stage is that the new environment is intriguing, but this perception tends to be screened and selective. The newcomer feels excited and stimulated by the newness and is likely to be curious and interested in the new school.

Disintegration. In the second stage the newcomer begins to feel significant differences between old and new environments. Contrasting cultural realities cannot be screened out. The newcomer feels increasing confusion and disorientation. Isolation and loneliness set in. The new student becomes depressed and withdraws.

Reintegration. In the third stage the differences between old and new environments become all-important. The new school culture is rejected. The newcomer feels angry, frustrated, and anxious. Attitudes of rebellion, suspicion, and hostility are exhibited. The new student may appear to be highly opinionated, usually preoccupied with likes and dislikes.

Autonomy. In the fourth stage a measure of balance is regained. Legitimate differences between old and new school cultures are recognized. The student feels less like an outsider, relaxes, and gains self-assurance. Confidence begins to return.

Independence. In the final stage differences between old and new environments are recognized and valued. Attitudes of trust, humor, and the full range of previous emotions are restored. The student becomes expressive, creative, and self-actualizing.

These stages provide a useful frame of reference for educators who deal with transient students. By understanding the progressive stages of the culture shock phenomenon, sensitive teachers, counselors, and administrators can help new students work through the stages and thus alleviate the severity of disorientation symptoms.

Academic Expectations

Another tension associated with the culture shock of moving to a new school is the matter of academic expectations. One of the respondents in the study I conducted of military children articulated the central concern. Now a 39-year-old human services administrator, this respondent wrote: "I always experienced fears as a child in moving that I hadn't learned as much in a previous school as I would be expected to know in a new school." Another respondent, now a 40-year-old paralegal, said: "Moving frequently, especially during high school . . . caused some problems in adjusting to a different school curriculum, primarily when a move was made during a school year."

Academic expectations are a concern to most transient students. Even young students feel anxious about "knowing enough" to fit into the appropriate grade or class at their new school. Highly transient students often recount horror stories of lost records, repeated lessons or classes, and even their high school graduation in jeopardy as a result of relocating to a new school with significantly different expectations. In some cases, delays in transit of official transcripts and other school records have caused students to be given inappropriate placements simply because personnel at the new school chose not to believe what new students or their parents told them about previous educational experiences.

Anxiety over a new school's academic expectations is reflected in such questions as, Will I be placed in the right grade? The right reading group? Will I know as much as the other kids in my class? Will I have to repeat courses I've already taken? Will I graduate on time? Anxiety over academic expectations adds one more layer to the culture shock already felt by students moving to a new community and school.

The Transient Student's Need to Belong

Children who move suffer the loss of social support systems. There-
fore, the first task in meeting the affective needs of transient students
is helping them to regain and rebuild those social support systems
in their new environment. As quickly as possible, newcomers need
to feel a sense of belonging. Once this basic need is fulfilled, it is
easier for new students to tackle academic tasks and to get on with
the business of learning.

When transient students, for whatever reasons, are unable to obtain membership in the new school culture, they are at risk of school
failure. Characteristics of at-risk students include the following:

- Frequent absences
- Delays in acquiring basic skills
- Failing grades
- Negative attitudes
- Inappropriate social interaction
- Expressions of negative self-concept
- Lack of motivation
- Poor work or study habits
- Inattention and forgetfulness

A transient student faced with impediments to membership in the
new school culture may exhibit one or more of these at-risk symptoms.
The impediment may be a lack of opportunities for positive interac-

tion with peers. Students with limited social skills may need the intervention of a teacher or counselor to help them find friends and develop a new peer support system.

Academic difficulties are also an impediment to membership. There may be conflict between social needs and pressures from home and school to achieve academic goals. Lack of peer support isolates newcomers from potential assistance. The student who has not yet established friendships in the new school may feel there is no one to turn to for help with academic assignments. Failing grades, especially for students who have been successful previously, tend to isolate them further from potentially supportive peers. New students also may need help to set priorities, to sort out their social needs and academic needs, and to plan ways to meet these needs in a balanced manner.

Finally, isolation is an impediment to belonging. Especially in large schools, the new student may see newly made friends only infrequently simply because of the size of the institution. Likewise in large attendance areas, school friends may live too far away to be visited outside of school. Social class and race are other factors that may contribute to isolation.

Developing a Sense of Community

Educators sensitive to the affective needs of transient students can take specific steps to help them gain a sense of community in the new culture. These steps involve helping them attain a measure of ownership in the new culture, providing them with many opportunities to participate in the work and play of the school, and ensuring success in social interaction and academic achievement. Following are some practical ways that educators can help new students achieve a sense of community in their new setting.

Attaining a Sense of Ownership. To help new students attain ownership in their new school, teachers need to intervene early. They need to demonstrate to the new student that he or she is a valued addition — and valued as a person — from the first moments in school. This means:

- Learning the student's name and pronouncing it correctly and asking how the student wishes to be addressed if a nickname is preferred. Particular attention should be paid to foreign students' names. For example, Vietnamese names are usually given last name first, middle name, and then first name. Vietnamese people are usually addressed by their first name.

- Learning something about cultural differences of the students and being sensitive to the differences when working with students.

- Providing opportunities for students to share information about their experiences and to exchange cultural information. These opportunities are as important for the student who moves from Texas to Wisconsin as for the refugee student from Cambodia.

- Helping new students develop realistic expectations for adjusting to the new school environment. Discussing the school culture in class and in private conversations enables newcomers to gain a sense of the school community and how they fit in.

To gain ownership in the school, new students must feel secure enough to set aside ego-protective mechanisms (withdrawal, aggressiveness, braggadocio) in order to adjust to the norms and values of the new setting. Students who are made to feel secure are better able to establish a social support system in the new school.

Opportunities for Participation. Schools can help newcomers become full participants in the school culture by making certain that they have opportunities to meet and interact with teachers, administrators and other students. This means:

- Providing personal introductions to teachers and administrators.

- Structuring instructional programs to meet varied needs so that newcomers "fit in" with the new academic peer group.

- Encouraging cooperative learning, both to diminish competition (which often keeps newcomers on the outside) and to build community among all students.

- Making new students aware of extracurricular activities and special programs and asking student leaders to invite them to participate.

- Examining placement and credit policies — especially at the high school level — to make sure that transient students are not victims of the records paper chase, where delays in receiving transcripts and cumulative records can put newcomers into academic limbo, or worse.

When new students are participating, they make new friends, they feel involved, they become part of the community.

Ensuring Success. Ownership and participation are part of the foundation for success, but schools can do more. Teachers who work with newcomers can help to ensure success not only in academic achievement but also in social adjustment by being sensitive to their affective needs. This means:

- Assessing new students' social skills and academic levels and working with them gradually to build on what they come with.

- Using a variety of teaching styles to accommodate students' varied learning styles. Limited-English-speaking students, in particular, benefit from instruction that includes nonverbal gestures and written material to supplement oral instruction.

- Emphasizing teamwork and cooperation, which build behavioral and academic support for newcomers. For example, using a buddy system helps the newcomer to integrate into the school community — and it works whether the student is in first grade or twelfth.

The adage, "Nothing succeeds like success," is particularly appropriate for helping the new student make the transition to a new school culture. Students who attain membership in the new school community rebuild their social support system and regain their self-confidence, thus strengthening their self-concept and setting in motion the positive attitudes and behaviors that enable them to achieve academic success. Any number of researchers have concluded that a student's self-concept is causally related to academic achievement (Bloom 1976; Purkey 1970).

Each change of school for the transient student presents a transition point — a point of risk — where the actions of the student, parents, and educators can set in motion either a positive or a negative spiral of affect. The challenge for those who work with transient students is to set in motion events that generate positive affect, which in turn leads to personal and academic success for the student.

Support Programs to Serve
the Affective Needs of Transient Students

Schools with high levels of student mobility need to develop formal programs to deal successfully with the affective needs of transient students. From a review of the literature and the author's own inquiries, several types of support programs are possible. These include sponsorships of new students and their families, peer support groups, mentors, individual and group counseling, and parent support groups. In addition, forward-looking school systems offer inservice programs to help staff better understand the special needs of transient students and their parents.

Sponsorships

The U.S. military offers a model that can be easily adapted by school systems. On many military installations incoming families are assigned a sponsor. The sponsor is someone who has lived or worked on the installation for a time and who can guide the newcomers through their first days and weeks. Often the sponsor becomes a first friend in the new location.

Schools can adapt the sponsorship model for new students by providing a student sponsor for every incoming student. This program might be a responsibility of the student council or other student service organization. The key is to make sure that each new student is met by the peer sponsor on arrival and that the sponsor is someone who is available and willing to take on the role of guide and friend. (At the secondary level, it is best if the sponsor has the same or similar class schedule.)

Again using the military model, schools can help parents adjust to the new community by providing sponsors for families. Parent-teacher organizations are a natural group to undertake this activity. If possible, family sponsors should be matched with newcomer families that have similar configurations and are in approximately the same social circumstances.

Peer Support Groups

Another support program is the peer support group. Cooperative learning and other types of classroom peer groups have been suggested earlier. In addition to these, more formal peer support groups for students with similar backgrounds can be organized. Such homogeneous peer groups are particularly valuable where there is a seasonal influx of new students, such as the children of migrant workers. Students with similar linguistic and cultural backgrounds may find security in a peer support group as they make the transition into the larger fabric of student life at the new school.

In schools with high turnover of mobile students, another function of peer support groups can be to provide on-going orientation to the school. With the help of counselors, teachers, and administrators, such groups can conduct periodic orientations throughout the year for newcomers who were not enrolled when the standard start-of-school orientation was conducted.

Mentors

A mentor is someone to whom a newcomer can turn for advice and support in a one-on-one, confidential relationship. Mentors usually are adults in some position of authority. They may be teachers, coaches, counselors, or administrators. The mentor is someone who touches base daily with the new student, says "Hello," checks on how the student is adjusting, and generally provides positive affective support.

A mentor also serves as the new student's advocate, making sure that records and official matters are taken care of, including matters of placement, school supplies, and even discipline. Mentors should be recruited from the official school staff. Peers cannot fulfill the responsibilities of effective mentoring.

Group and Individual Counseling

Both group and individual counseling are an important component of the support system for newcomers. The school counselor's role can range from simply being a good listener to developing peer and mentor programs, working with parent groups, providing inservice training for staff, and being a program leader and change agent.

Counselors often are called on to work directly with groups or to arrange for leadership by some other staff member, for example, a bilingual teacher. They may also structure counseling groups in a variety of configurations: all newcomers, newcomers and "oldtimers," military and civilian, and so on. Effective counseling programs for transient students anticipate problems before they reach crisis levels.

Parent Support Groups

Counselors can also be instrumental in developing parent support group programs. A number of researchers have suggested that programs in parenting may be particularly useful for the population groups most often characterized as mobile or transient. This is another area where counselors, working with teachers, administrators, parent organizations, and other community support agencies, can provide leadership.

Findings at the Center for Demographic Studies (1984) show that military servicemen are more likely to marry earlier and start their families at a younger age than their civilian counterparts. Thus, young military families may be less prepared for the demands of parenthood and would be receptive to programs in parenting education. Similarly, some immigrant groups, for example, Southeast Asians, tend to follow a pattern of early marriage and childbearing. These groups, too, could be offered parenting education as one component of an overall program designed to address the affective needs of transient students and their families.

Ten Ways of Serving the Affective Needs of Transient Students

In the way of summary, what follows is a list of 10 specific actions a school can take as a starting point in meeting the affective needs of transient students.

1. Each new student will be assigned a peer sponsor whose role will be to orient the newcomer to the social and procedural aspects of the school and to help the newcomer make new friends.
2. Each new family will be assigned a family sponsor whose role is to acquaint the family with the community and to help family members make friends in their new surroundings.
3. Each new student will be assigned a faculty mentor whose principal roles are to assist the student with the academic aspects of the school and to function as an advocate for the new student.
4. School leaders will conduct periodic orientation programs for new students who enter at various times throughout the year.
5. School counselors will schedule regular sessions to assist new students in adjusting to the new school.
6. School leaders will develop support groups for new students involving a variety of configurations based on their adjustment needs.
7. School leaders will develop support groups for new parents that provide orientation and information.

8. School leaders will provide parenting education programs when warranted for the parents of transient students.
9. School leaders will encourage educators and parent organizations to take an active role in the orientation and involvement of newcomers to the school district.
10. School leaders will develop inservice training programs to educate staff about the characteristics and needs of transient children and their families.

References

Adler, Peter. "Transitional Experience: An Alternative View of Culture Shock." *Journal of Humanistic Psychology* (Fall 1975): pp. 13-23.

Barna, LaRay. *How Culture Shock Affects Communication*. Paper presented at the Communication Association of the Pacific annual convention, Kobe, Japan, 1976.

Bloom, Benjamin. *Human Characteristics and School Learning*. New York: McGraw-Hill, 1976.

Calkins, Lucy. *The Art of Teaching Writing*. Portsmouth, N.H. : Heinemann, 1986.

Center for Demographic Studies. *Military Families: Do They Differ from Their Civilian Counterparts?* Washington, D.C.: U.S. Bureau of the Census, 1984.

Coles, Robert. *Uprooted Children: The Early Life of Migrant Farm Workers*. Pittsburgh, Pa.: University of Pittsburgh Press, 1970.

Hunter, Edna, and Hickman, Robert. *As Parents Go, So Go the Children: The Adjustment and Development of Military Children*. San Diego: U.S. International University, June 1981. DTIC ADA107347

Khleif, Bud. "The Military Dependent as a Stranger in Public Schools." *Sociologia Internationals* 16, no. 1-2 (1978): 153-62.

Packard, Vance. *A Nation of Strangers*. New York: David McKay, 1972.

Pisano, Marina. "Working Wives Break Military Unwritten Rule." *Sunday Express-News*, San Antonio, Texas, pp. 2E-3E, 19 September 1982.

Purkey, W. *Self-Concept and School Achievement*. Englewood Cliffs, N.J.: Prentice-Hall, 1970.

Additional Resources

Readers interested in understanding and working effectively with transient students and their families will find the following books helpful.

Ashabranner, Brent. *Dark Harvest: Migrant Farmworkers in America*. New York: Dodd, Mead & Company, 1985.

Carroll, Raymonde. *Cultural Misunderstandings: The French-American Experience*. Chicago: University of Chicago Press, 1988.

Lewis, Tom, and Jungman, Robert. *On Being Foreign: Culture Shock in Short Fiction*. Yarmouth, Maine: Intercultural Press, 1986.

Nida, Patricia C., and Heller, Wendy M. *The Teenager's Survival Guide to Moving*. New York: Atheneum, 1985.

The following newsletters also provide useful information:

Military Family
Office of the Assistant Secretary of Defense (Force Management and Personnel)
Military Family Resource Center
Ballston Centre Tower Three, Suite 903
4015 Wilson Boulevard
Arlington, VA 22203-5190

NCBE Forum
National Clearinghouse for Bilingual Education
8737 Colesville Road, Suite 900
Silver Spring, MD 20910

DEMCO